How Does TAP WATER Work?

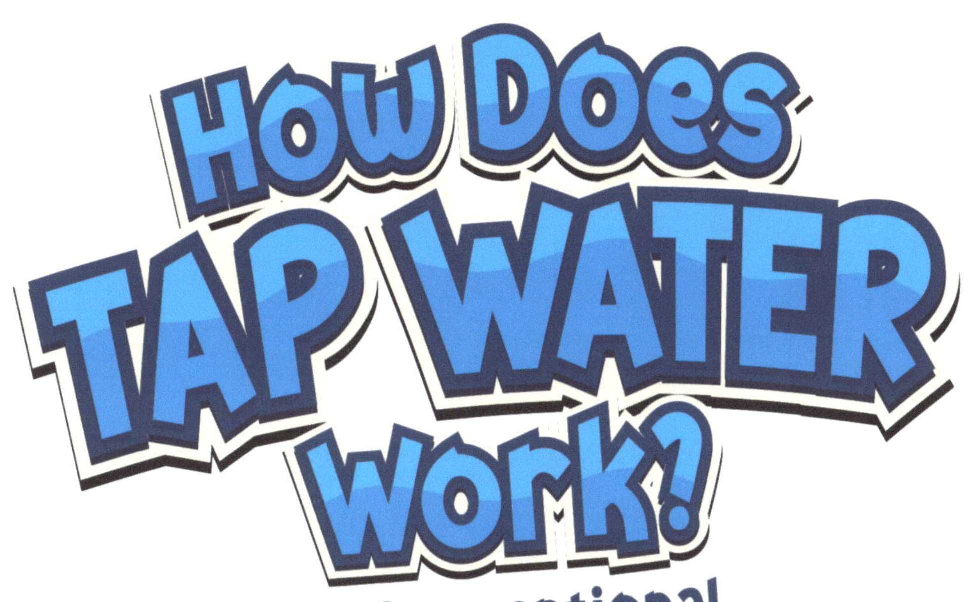

The Conventional Water Treatment Process

by Darrell A. King

How Does Tap Water Work
The Conventional Water Treatment Process
by Darrell A. King

Illustrations provided by Marlon at GetYourBookIllustrations
www.getyourbookillustrations.com

Copyright 2026 by Lively Hope Publishers, LLC
www.howdoestapwaterwork.com

All Rights Reserved

Published By Lively Hope Publishers, LLC
www.livelyhopepublishers.com

Hardback ISBN-13:   979-8-9952259-3-5
Paperback ISBN-13:   979-8-9952259-4-2
ebook ISBN-13:   979-8-9952259-2-8

First Edition
Printed in USA

Dedication

I thank God for inspiring me to write this book. I would like to thank my beautiful wife for her love, patience, support and understanding. You are my best friend. Thank you to my children, parents, and siblings, who have always been supportive of me. I would also like to thank the many water industry professionals and colleagues that I have worked with throughout the years.

Below is a note from my youngest daughter after she tasted the tap water at the water treatment facility that I managed.

"Can I have a cup of water Daddy"?

"Sure, you can sweetheart".

While filling the cup his daughter asks, "How Does Tap Water Work"?

Much of the fresh water on earth is frozen and therefore not able to be used. The Great Lakes (Superior, Michigan, Huron, Erie, and Ontario) on the other hand are usable and are located in the United States and Canada.

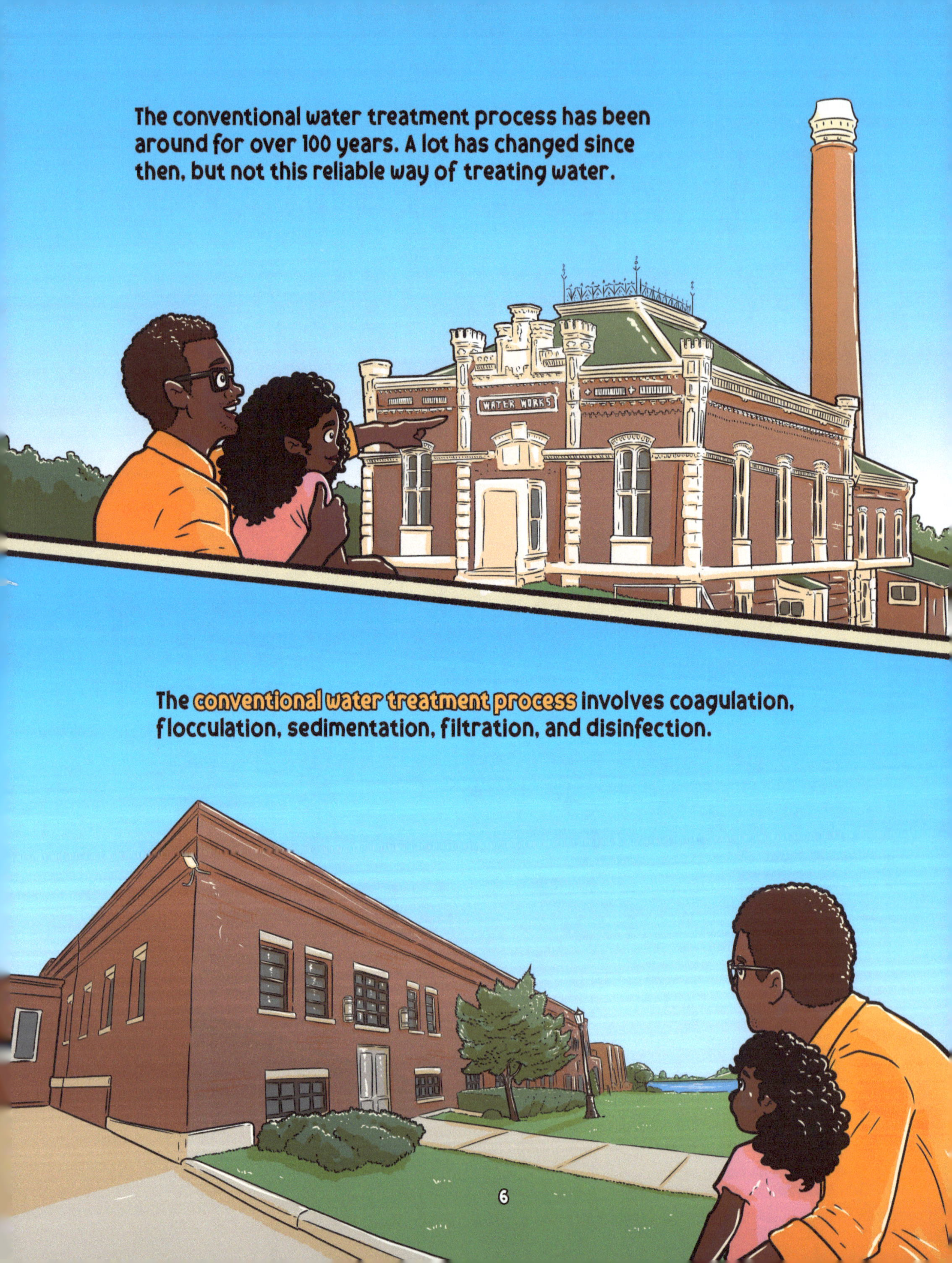

The conventional water treatment process has been around for over 100 years. A lot has changed since then, but not this reliable way of treating water.

The conventional water treatment process involves coagulation, flocculation, sedimentation, filtration, and disinfection.

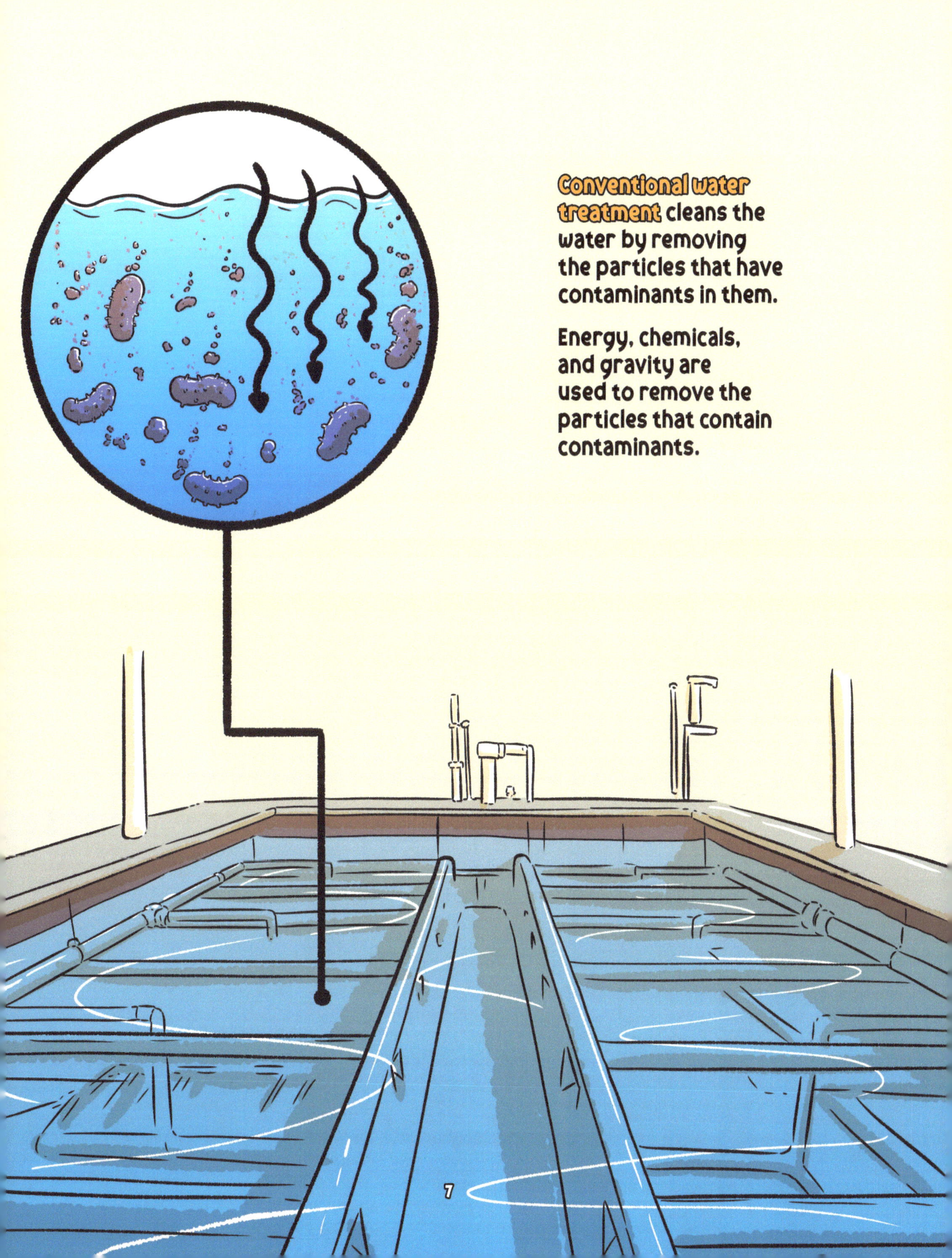

Conventional water treatment cleans the water by removing the particles that have contaminants in them.

Energy, chemicals, and gravity are used to remove the particles that contain contaminants.

Far out and deep in the lake (Lake Michigan for example) are intake structures (upturned cones). This is how raw/untreated source water is drawn from the lake into a water treatment plant.

At the end of the intake pipes, sometimes a wooden crib is installed on the intake upturned cone to protect the structure. The intake system is designed to slow the velocity of the water flow to reduce the risk of icing and fish from being sucked into the water treatment plant.

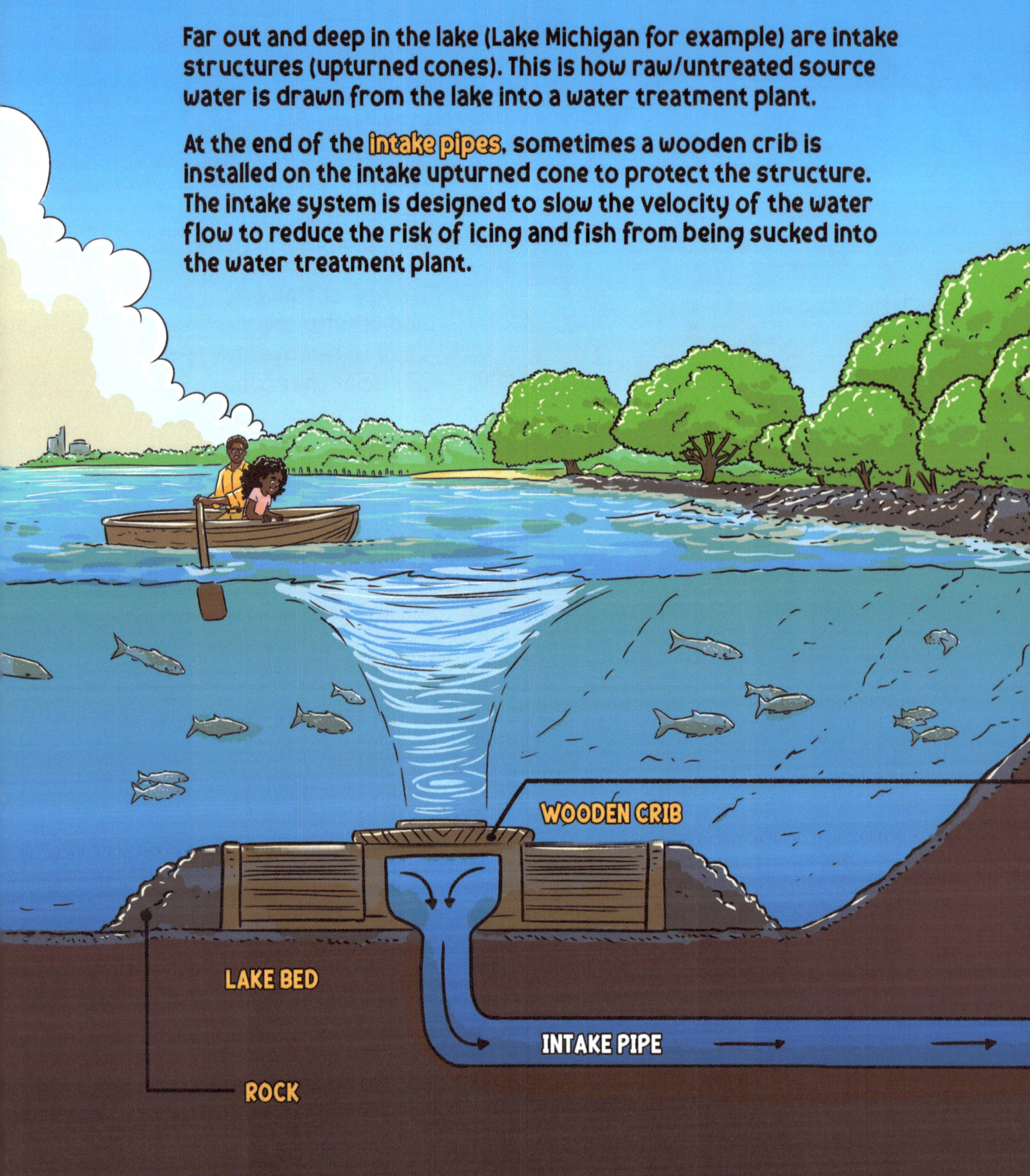

PUMP
STATION
WET
WELL
WOODEN CRIB
INTAKE PIPE
OUTLET PIPE
TREATMENT
PLANT

The intakes are inspected during the summer months when the water temperature is the warmest by certified divers. These inspections are done to perform maintenance, repairs, and ensure the intakes are in good condition.

There are contaminants that can be present in the raw water such as litter, dirt, clay, chemicals, bacteria, and parasites like giardia, and cryptosporidium.

Cryptosporidium has a thick outer shell that protects it from disinfection chemicals like chlorine, so it has to be removed another way.

The water flows into the intake wells by gravity. Screens are sometimes installed on top of the well structures to remove debris from entering the low lift pumps, which can cause damage to the pump's impeller.

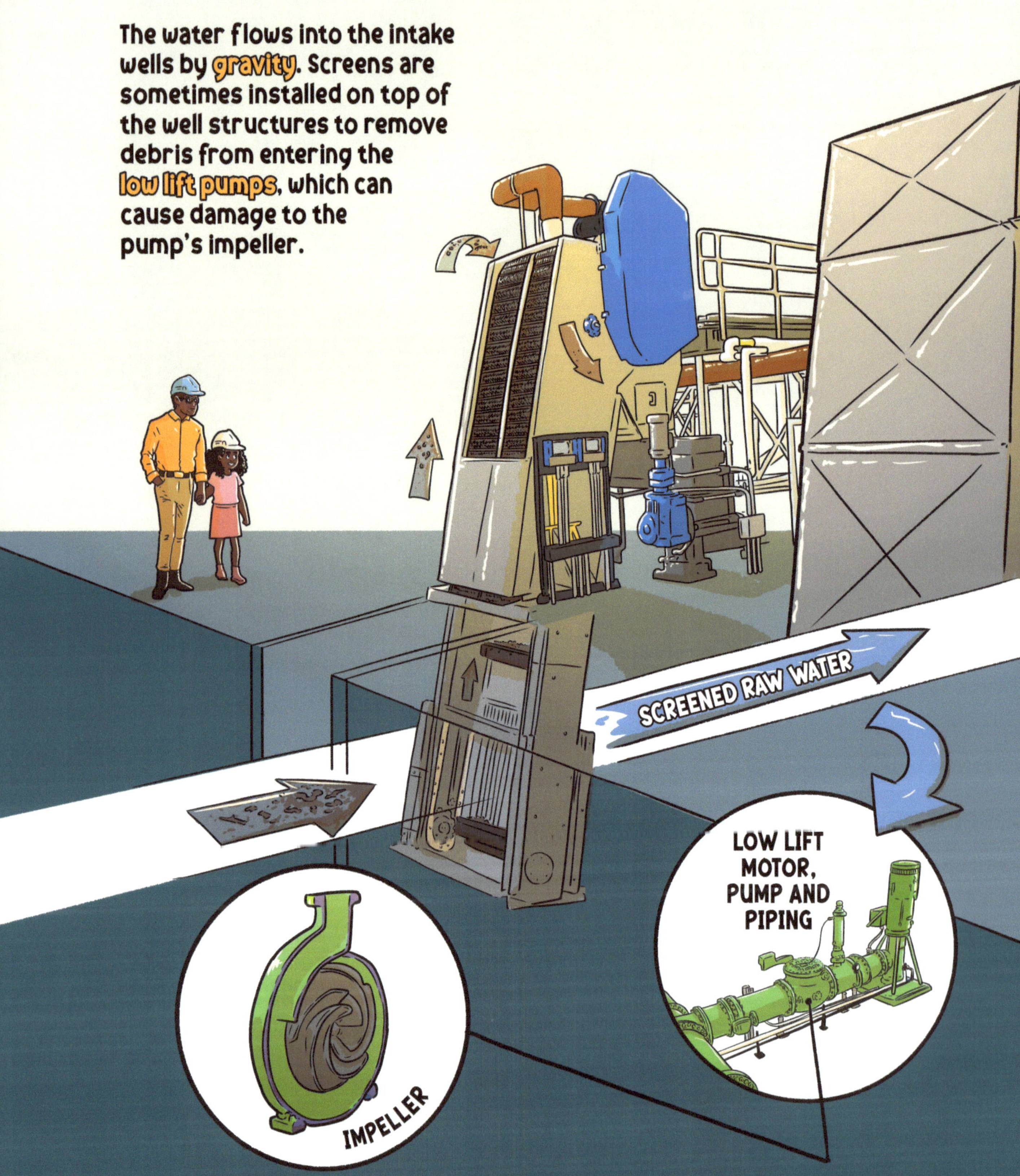

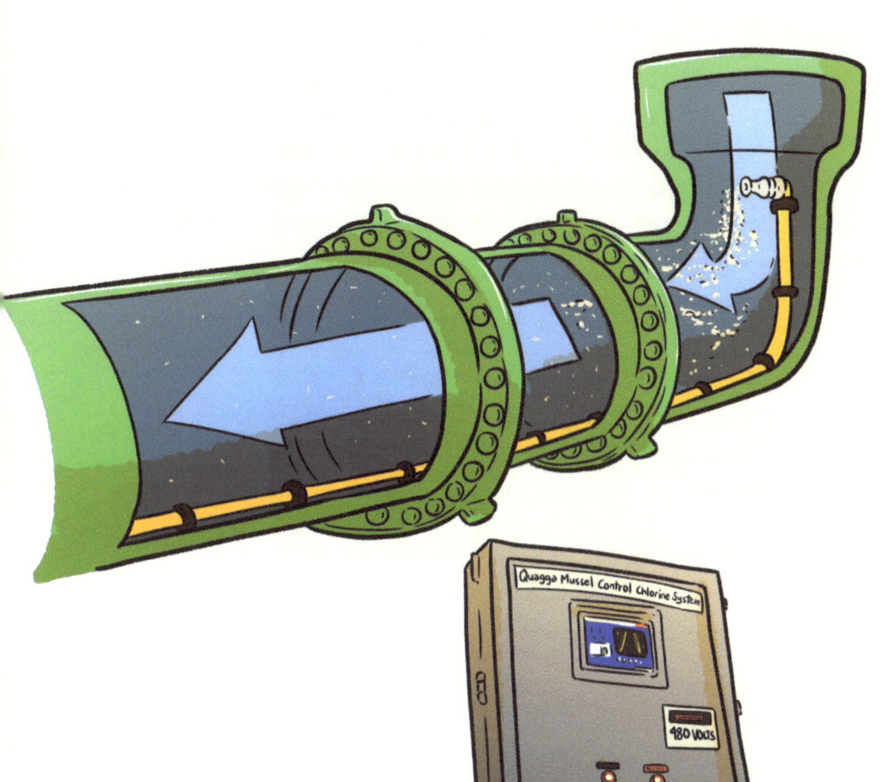

During the spring, summer, and fall seasons chlorine can be fed at the intakes through tubes that help control quagga mussel colonization. This occurs when the water temperature reaches 49 degrees Fahrenheit.

Quagga mussels are an invasive species that can clog the intake structures and prevent water from entering the water treatment plant.

The quagga mussels most likely arrived in the Great Lakes and other bodies of water from the ballast water of ocean ships that sailed from Europe.

The low lift pumps are used to move the raw water from the intake wells and lift the raw water into the rapid mix chamber to start the treatment process. The water flows by gravity through the remaining treatment processes.

Treatment starts in the rapid mix chamber where coagulants such as aluminum sulfate (alum) and a cationic polymer are added to the water. This is where particles begin to be removed due to the coagulation process.

The particles in the lake, called colloids, have negative charges that causes them to repel one another. The repelling force is due to zeta potential.

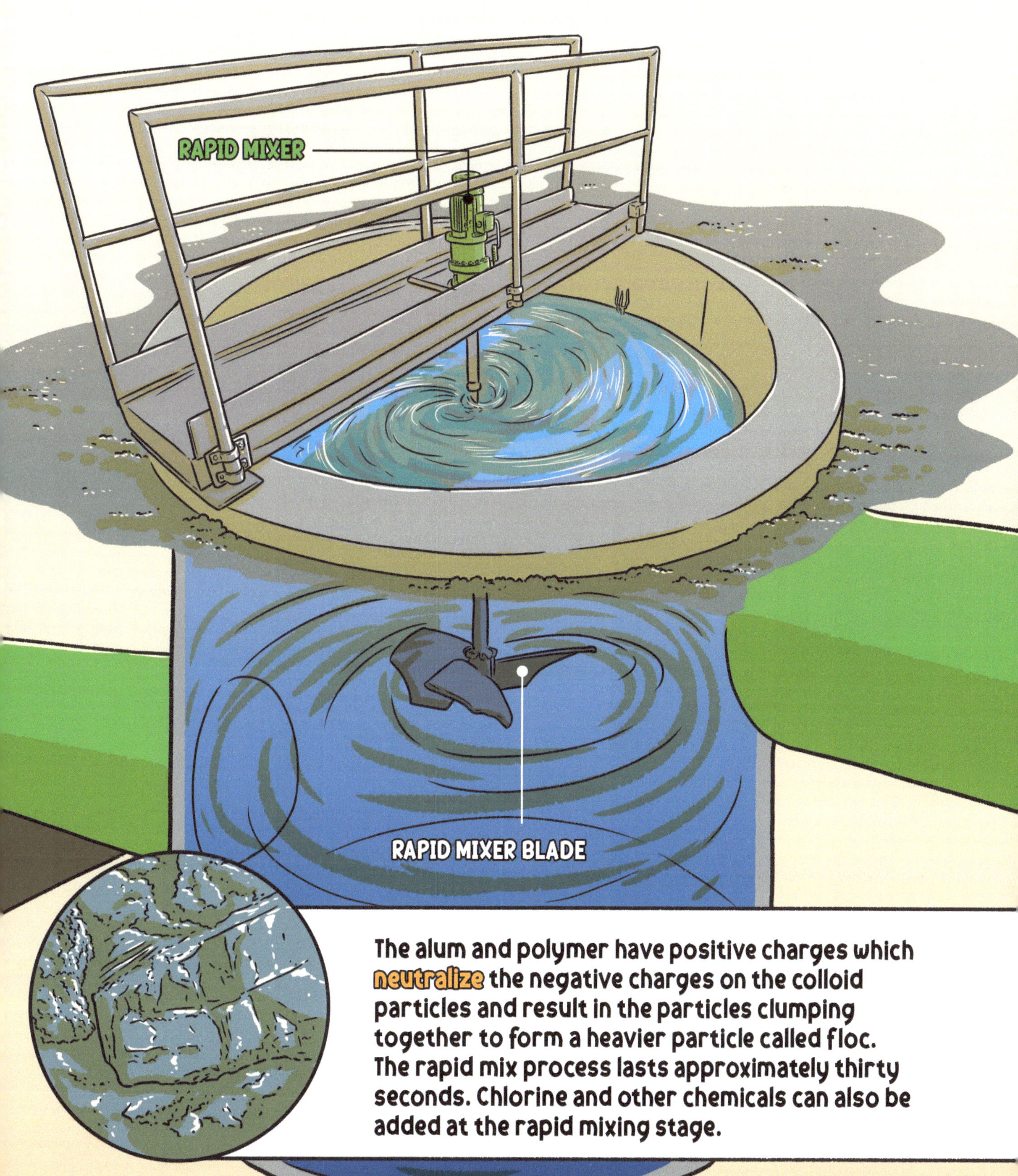

The alum and polymer have positive charges which neutralize the negative charges on the colloid particles and result in the particles clumping together to form a heavier particle called floc. The rapid mix process lasts approximately thirty seconds. Chlorine and other chemicals can also be added at the rapid mixing stage.

Following the rapid mix process, the water goes to the **flocculation**/ slow mix tank. The water is gently mixed by large paddles to allow the floc to become bigger and heavier. This process can last approximately one hour.

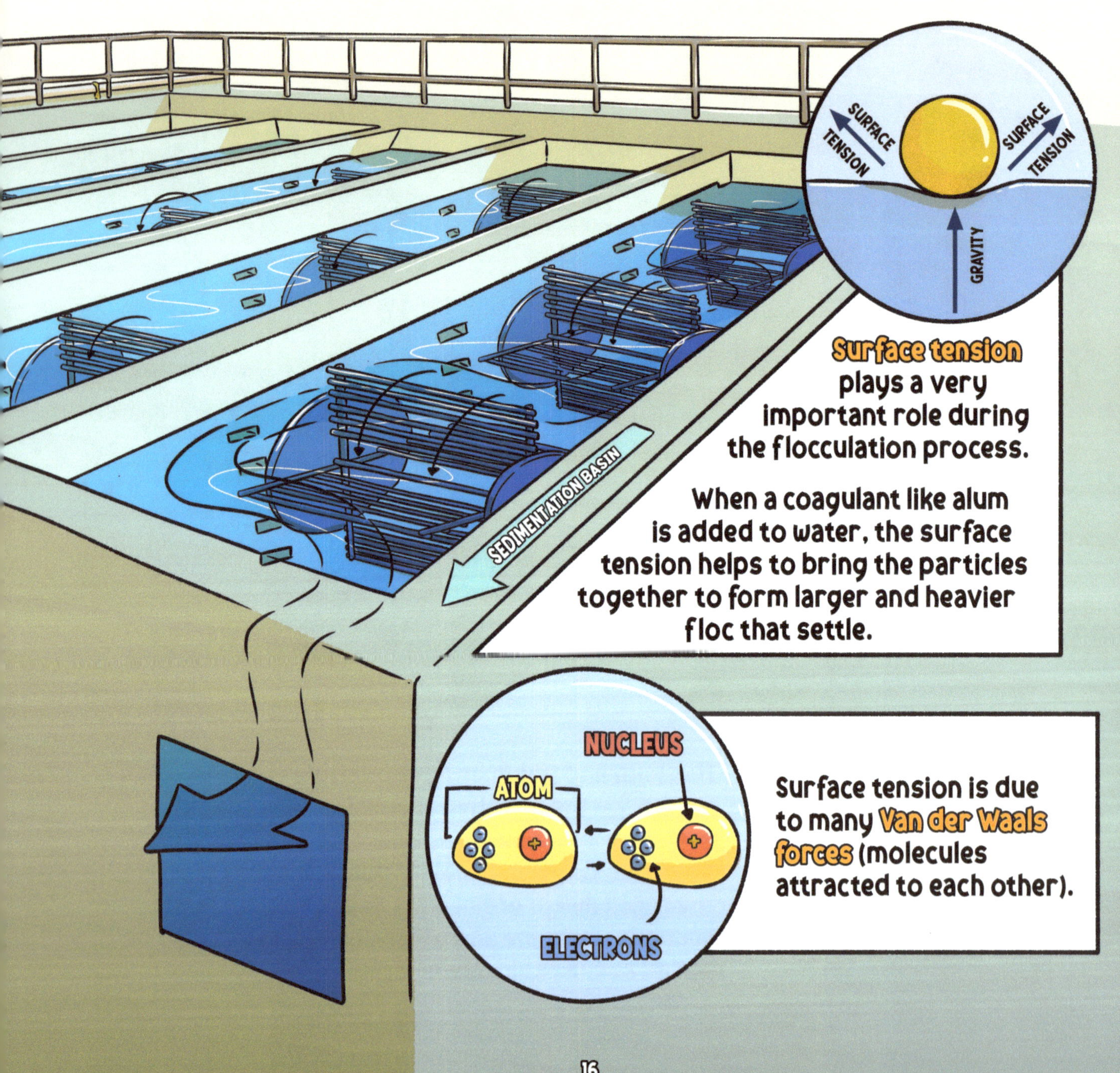

Surface tension plays a very important role during the flocculation process.

When a coagulant like alum is added to water, the surface tension helps to bring the particles together to form larger and heavier floc that settle.

Surface tension is due to many **Van der Waals forces** (molecules attracted to each other).

Following flocculation/slow mixing, the water goes to the sedimentation basin. This is a slow process and can take four hours or more for the floc to sink and settle to the bottom of the settling chamber.

This process removes over 90% of the floc. Gravity plays a key part of this process. This saves lots of energy which reduces the cost of treating the water. The flocculation and sedimentation processes are where the parasite cryptosporidium would be removed if it was present in the raw/ untreated water.

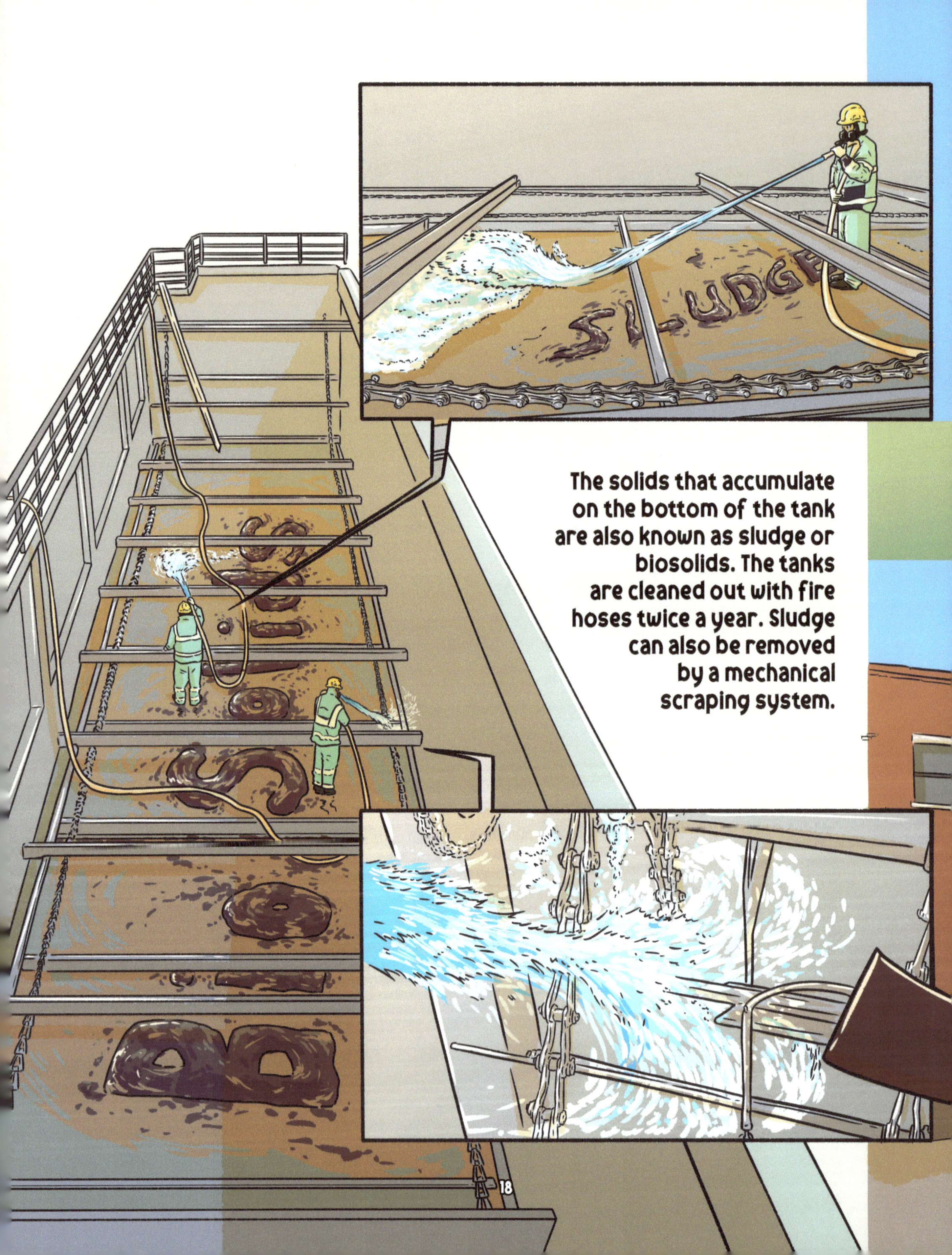

The solids that accumulate on the bottom of the tank are also known as sludge or biosolids. The tanks are cleaned out with fire hoses twice a year. Sludge can also be removed by a mechanical scraping system.

The sludge/biosolids can be disposed of by using a centrifuge or pumped to a wastewater facility for treatment and disposal. The centrifuge separates water from the sludge/biosolids. The biosolids can then be sent to a landfill using large trucks or used for farms, golf courses, highway shoulders, and other sustainable uses.

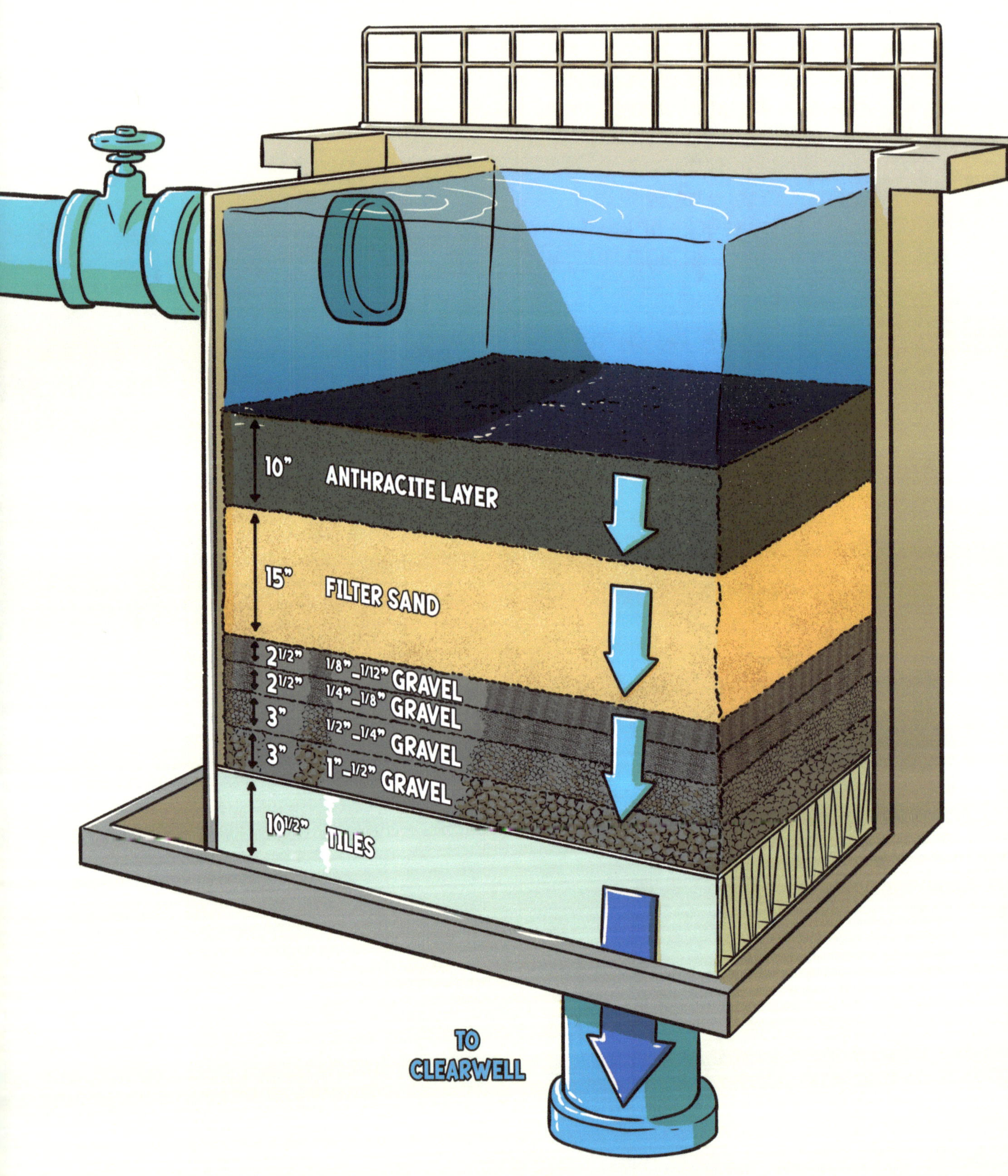

10"   ANTHRACITE LAYER
15"   FILTER SAND
2 1/2"   1/8"–1/12" GRAVEL
2 1/2"   1/4"–1/8" GRAVEL
3"   1/2"–1/4" GRAVEL
3"   1"–1/2" GRAVEL
10 1/2"   TILES
TO CLEARWELL

Following the sedimentation process, the water flows by gravity into the filters. This is the filtration process.

To protect the drinking water from sickness and disease-causing **microorganisms**, the United States government created the Surface Water Treatment Rule (SWTR).

The filters contain media that have a layer of anthracite, and sand. The filters can also have layers of different sizes of stones underneath the anthracite and sand. This media is referred to as an adsorbent. The multimedia filters remove the remaining floc that didn't settle out during the sedimentation process. The floc sticks to the surface of the adsorbent. This process is called **adsorption**.

THE SURFACE WATER TREATMENT RULE (SWTR)

The SWTR requires water treatment facilities that use surface water (The Great Lakes for example) as its source, to provide both filtration and disinfection treatment processes.

As water passes through the filters (from top to bottom) the filtered water enters the under-drain system, which is located at the bottom of the filter. Filter back washing occurs frequently using tap water by reversing the flow of water through a filter to clean it and remove trapped debris. This process requires energy. About ten percent of the backwash water can be sent to the beginning of the treatment process and retreated.

Filter backwashing can be based on filter runtime, bottom filter turbidity, filter **loss of head** (requires increased pressure to filter the water), or other factors that have been determined by the plant responsible operator in charge of water quality.

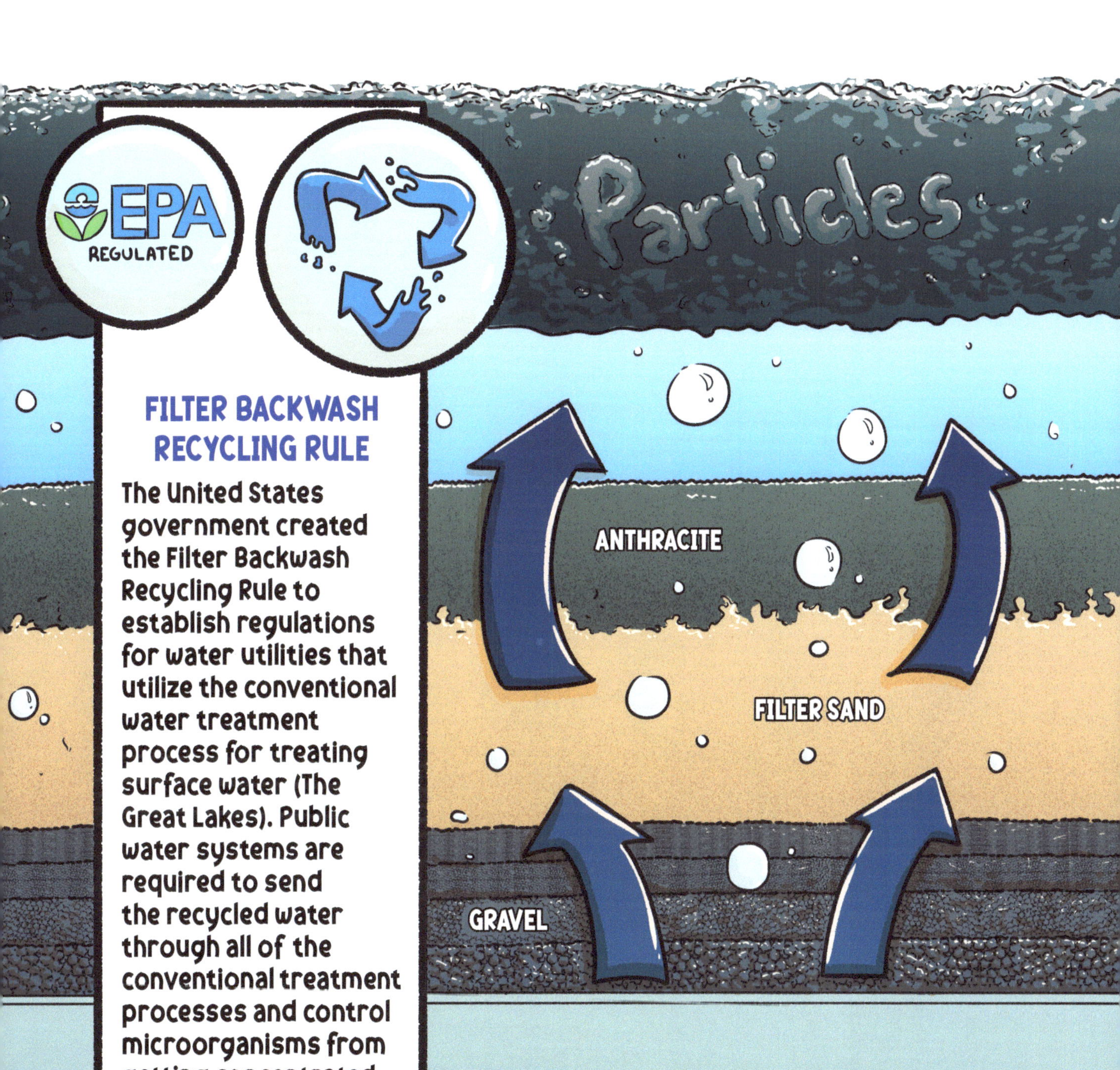
EPA
REGULATED
Particles
FILTER BACKWASH
RECYCLING RULE
The United States government created the Filter Backwash Recycling Rule to establish regulations for water utilities that utilize the conventional water treatment process for treating surface water (The Great Lakes). Public water systems are required to send the recycled water through all of the conventional treatment processes and control microorganisms from getting concentrated.
ANTHRACITE
FILTER SAND
GRAVEL

After filtration, chlorine is added to the water to prevent the spread of disease caused by bacteria and other organisms. This process is called disinfection. The addition of chlorine to the water must be done carefully to prevent the creation of high levels of disinfection byproducts. These byproducts have been known to increase the risk of cancer.

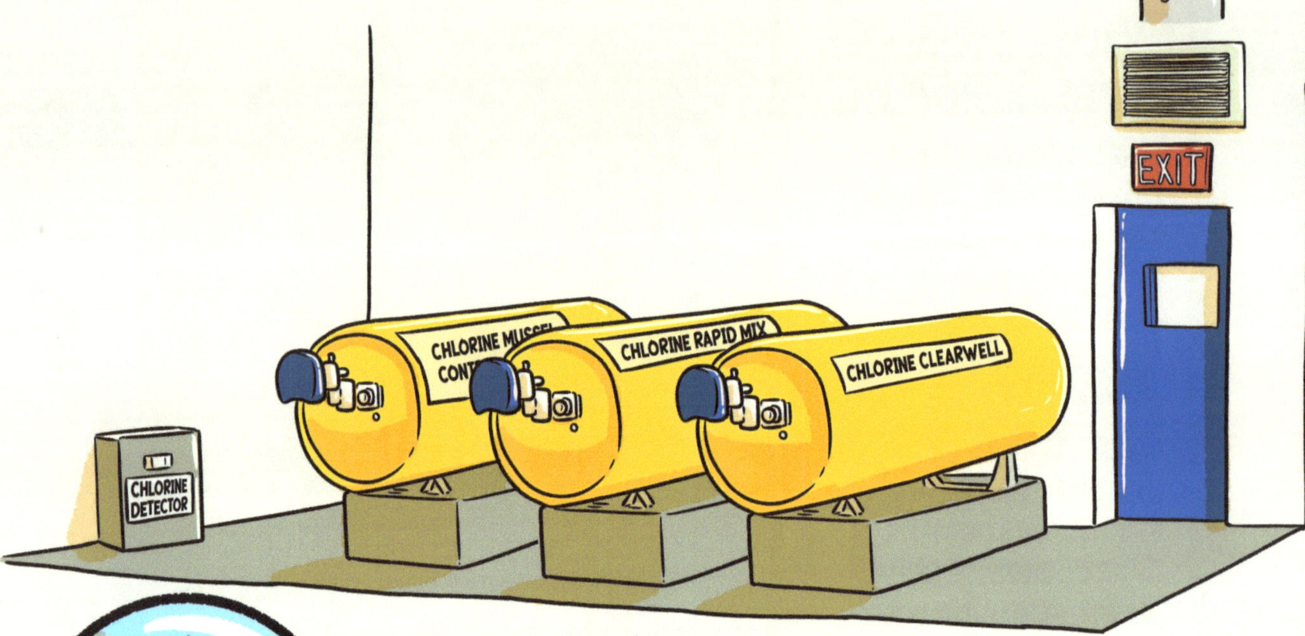

DISINFECTION BYPRODUCTS RULE (DBPR)

The United States government created the Disinfection Byproducts Rule (DBPR), which establishes maximum contaminant levels for disinfection byproducts (DBPs) in drinking water. DBPs are created when disinfectants react with organic matter (leaves, algae, dead insects, fish waste, and others) in the water. DBPs are known to increase the risk for cancer if exposure occurs at certain levels.

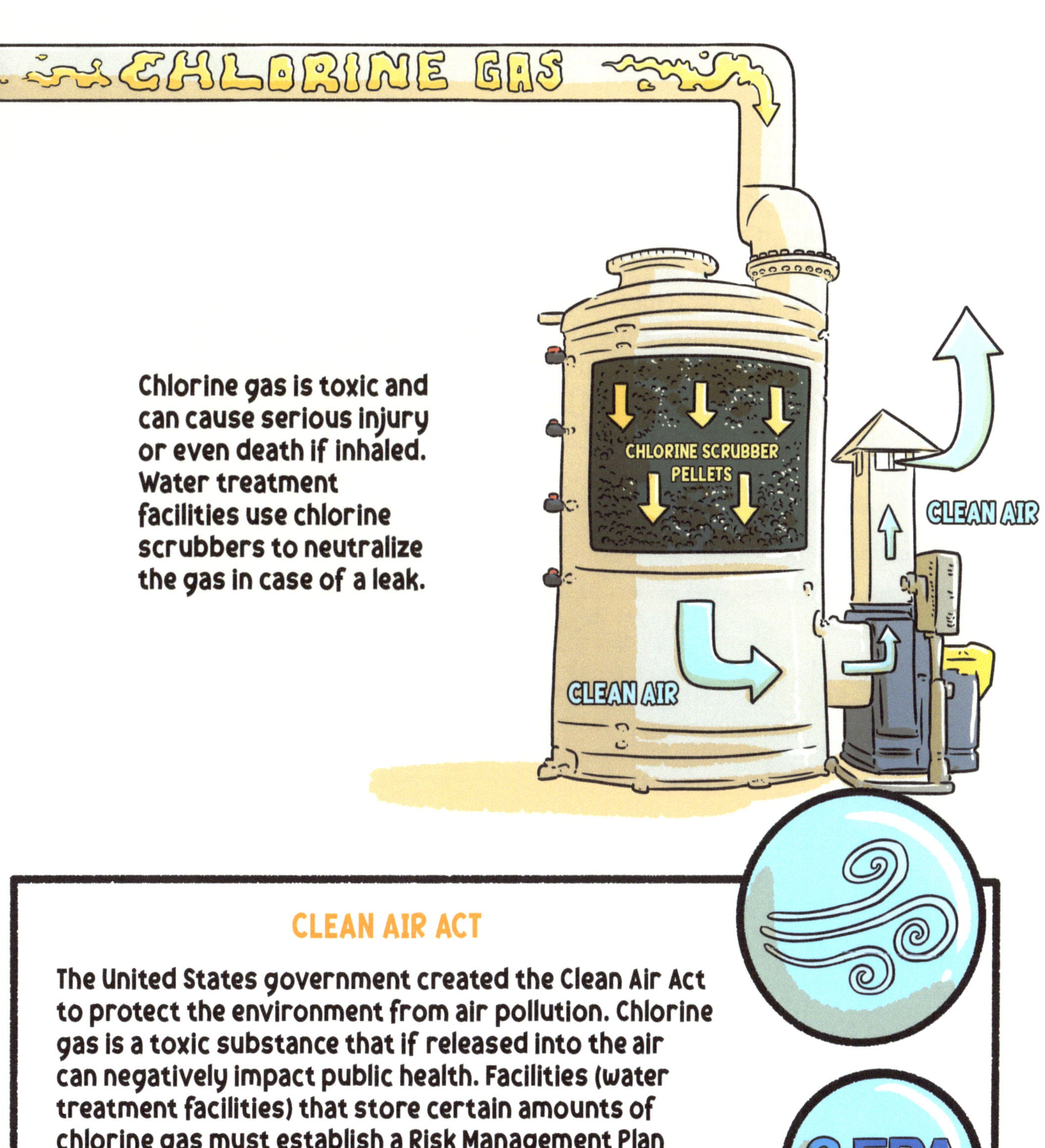

Chlorine gas is toxic and can cause serious injury or even death if inhaled. Water treatment facilities use chlorine scrubbers to neutralize the gas in case of a leak.

CLEAN AIR ACT

The United States government created the Clean Air Act to protect the environment from air pollution. Chlorine gas is a toxic substance that if released into the air can negatively impact public health. Facilities (water treatment facilities) that store certain amounts of chlorine gas must establish a Risk Management Plan (RMP) to properly manage the gas and reduce the risk of a release into the air.

The water then flows into underground storage tanks called **clearwells**. A minimum chlorine contact time of 60 minutes must be provided before pumping the water into the community to ensure proper disinfection occurred. The clearwells are massive concrete tanks with multiple pillars that support the structure. Once the water enters the clearwell, it has been successfully treated and is now finished drinking water/potable. The finished water must achieve certain turbidity levels.

Turbidity is a measure of the cloudiness of water. It is used to indicate water quality and if the treatment process was effective.

NATIONAL PRIMARY DRINKING WATER REGULATIONS

The United States government created the National Primary Drinking Water Regulations that require water systems to comply with certain standards and perform treatment techniques that prevent exceeding enforceable maximum contaminant levels in drinking water.

A **corrosion inhibitor** (orthophosphate) can be introduced into the water in the clearwells or as water is pumped into the **distribution system**. This helps prevent metals such as lead, copper, or galvanized steel from leaching into the water by creating a white protective coating on the inner surfaces of the pipes. Leaching usually occurs when the water has been sitting in the pipes for six hours or more.

LEAD AND COPPER RULE REVISION (LCRR)

The United States government created the Lead and Copper Rule Revision (LCRR) to better protect public health, especially children, from the harmful effects of both lead and copper exposure in the drinking water. This regulation calls for corrosion control optimization studies, updated sampling procedures and frequencies, find and fix requirements, public outreach, and lead service line replacements.

The **high lift pumps** pump the water out of the clearwells to homes, schools, churches, and businesses throughout the distribution system. The high lift pumps use **energy** (electricity) to distribute the water. These pumps can also use fossil fuel energy sources such as natural gas, diesel, or renewable energy sources (wind, solar) for backup in case of an electrical power outage.

Mechanics perform regular maintenance on the high lift pumps to ensure they function properly.

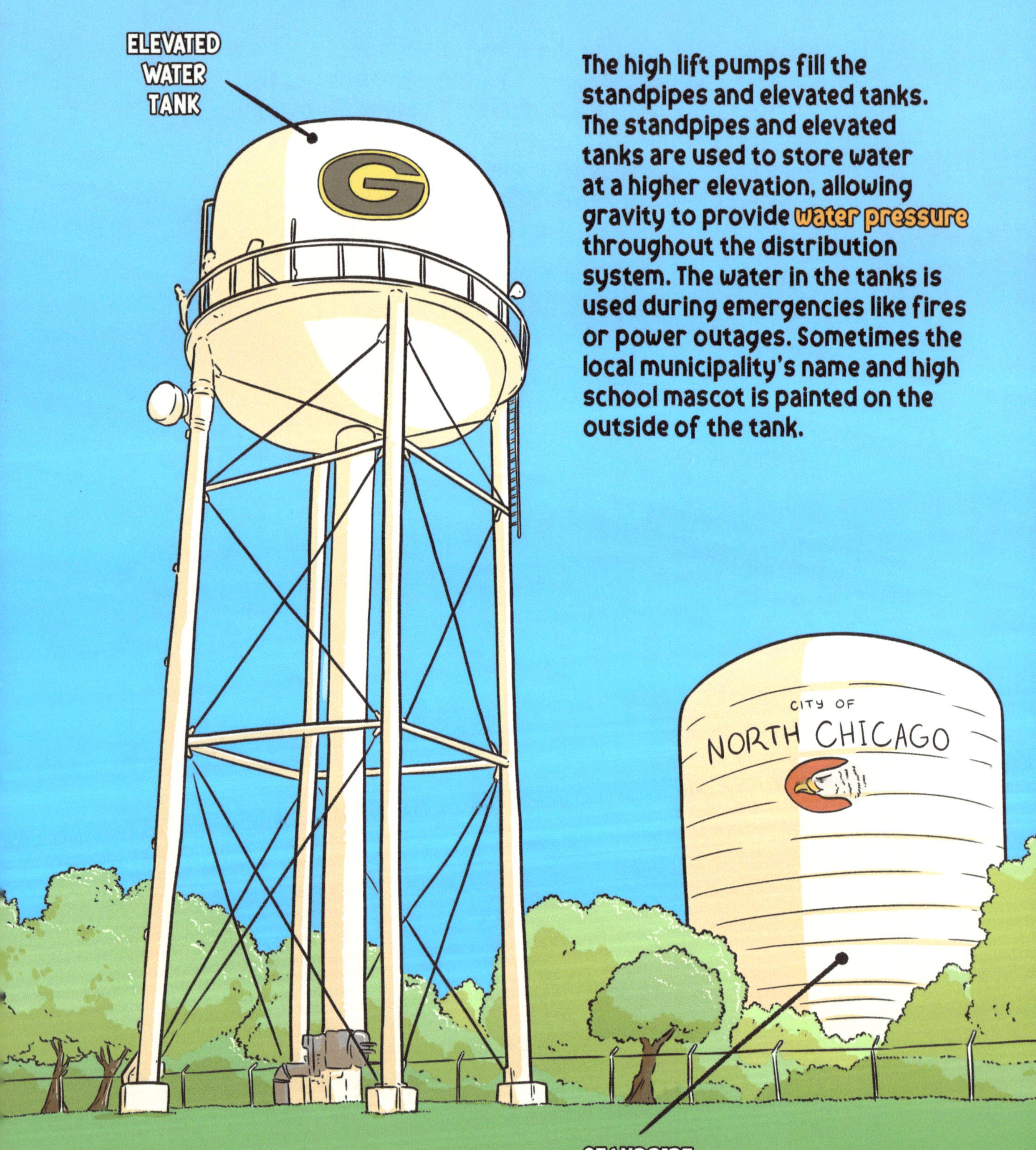

The high lift pumps fill the standpipes and elevated tanks. The standpipes and elevated tanks are used to store water at a higher elevation, allowing gravity to provide water pressure throughout the distribution system. The water in the tanks is used during emergencies like fires or power outages. Sometimes the local municipality's name and high school mascot is painted on the outside of the tank.

The high lift pumps also provide pressure that sends the water throughout the community through an underground network of pipes called water mains. Fire hydrants are connected to the water mains, so the brave firefighters are able to fight fires with pressurized water.

These water mains are used to deliver the water to the street that people live on. Water service pipes are connected to the water mains and extend into each house. Water meters are used to measure the amount of water used at each house. The water meter can be in a meter pit in the parkway or on the inside of the house in the basement or other location.

Water operators are always monitoring the treatment process and distribution system using a **Supervisory Control and Data Acquisition (SCADA)** system from the control room to ensure everything goes smoothly. Every hour they also perform rounds throughout the treatment plant to check on equipment and conduct water quality tests at each stage of the process. Operators can also monitor video surveillance cameras to ensure the security of the facility.

Continuous monitoring devices measure various water quality levels like chlorine and turbidity and transmit the data to the SCADA system every fifteen minutes.

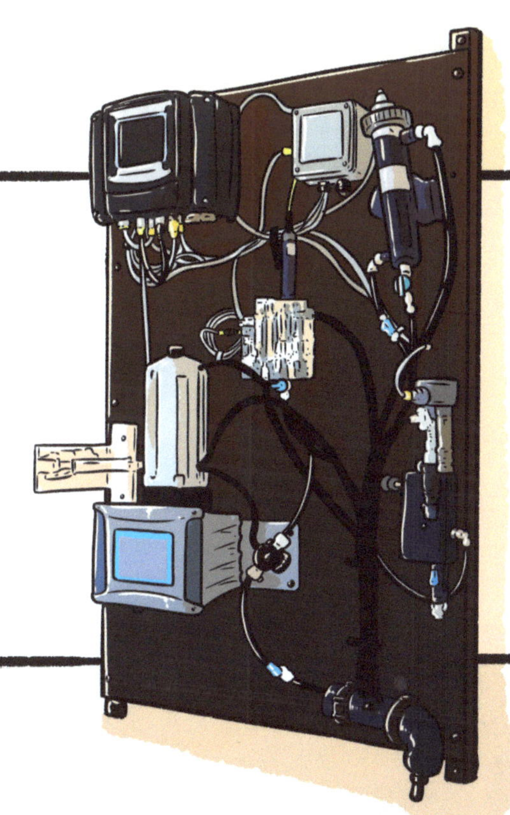

The amount of water pumped throughout the distribution system is determined by the demand or the amount of water needed by the community at a specific time. The amount pumped is represented as million gallons per day (MGD). This demand changes throughout the day and night.

The water quality laboratory analysts, like the Chemist, perform tests to ensure the water quality meets all standards. Included in these tests are total coliform testing. Total coliforms are harmless bacteria that if detected can indicate the presence of more harmful bacteria like E. Coli.

REVISED TOTAL COLIFORM RULE

The United States government created the Revised Total Coliform Rule to protect the drinking water from bacterial contamination outbreaks. This rule replaces the previous Total Coliform Rule that was passed in 1989. Public water supplies are required to perform coliform testing every month throughout the drinking water distribution system as well as test for chlorine residuals at each approved site. The number of required coliform testing sites is dependent upon the population of the community being served by the water supply.

Sometimes the water mains break, and workers must go out and repair them to prevent water from being wasted and causing damage. Repairs are performed during the day and at night. This can occur on weekends and holidays. Water workers are first responders and always ready!

Water is not treated the same way everywhere because contaminants in the source water are different. Treatment facilities can combine conventional treatment with membrane treatment or use only membranes as the primary treatment. Source water can come from lakes, rivers, and even the ocean. Source water can also come from the ground where it is pumped out of aquifers.

There are lots of water industry professionals: laborers, mechanics, laboratory technicians, water operators, engineers, utility managers, geographic information system (GIS) technicians, plumbers, customer service specialists, attorneys, financial specialists, and more.

WATER TREATMENT FACILITY
START
FINISH
Inside the house are pipes that are connected to sinks and faucets. When you turn on the faucet, the pressurized tap water comes out. Water is being treated, tested, and pumped twenty-four hours a day, and seven days a week.

From start to finish, the conventional water treatment process can last up to 5 hours or more depending on the size, design of the treatment plant, raw water quality, amount of water being treated, pumped, and operational procedures.

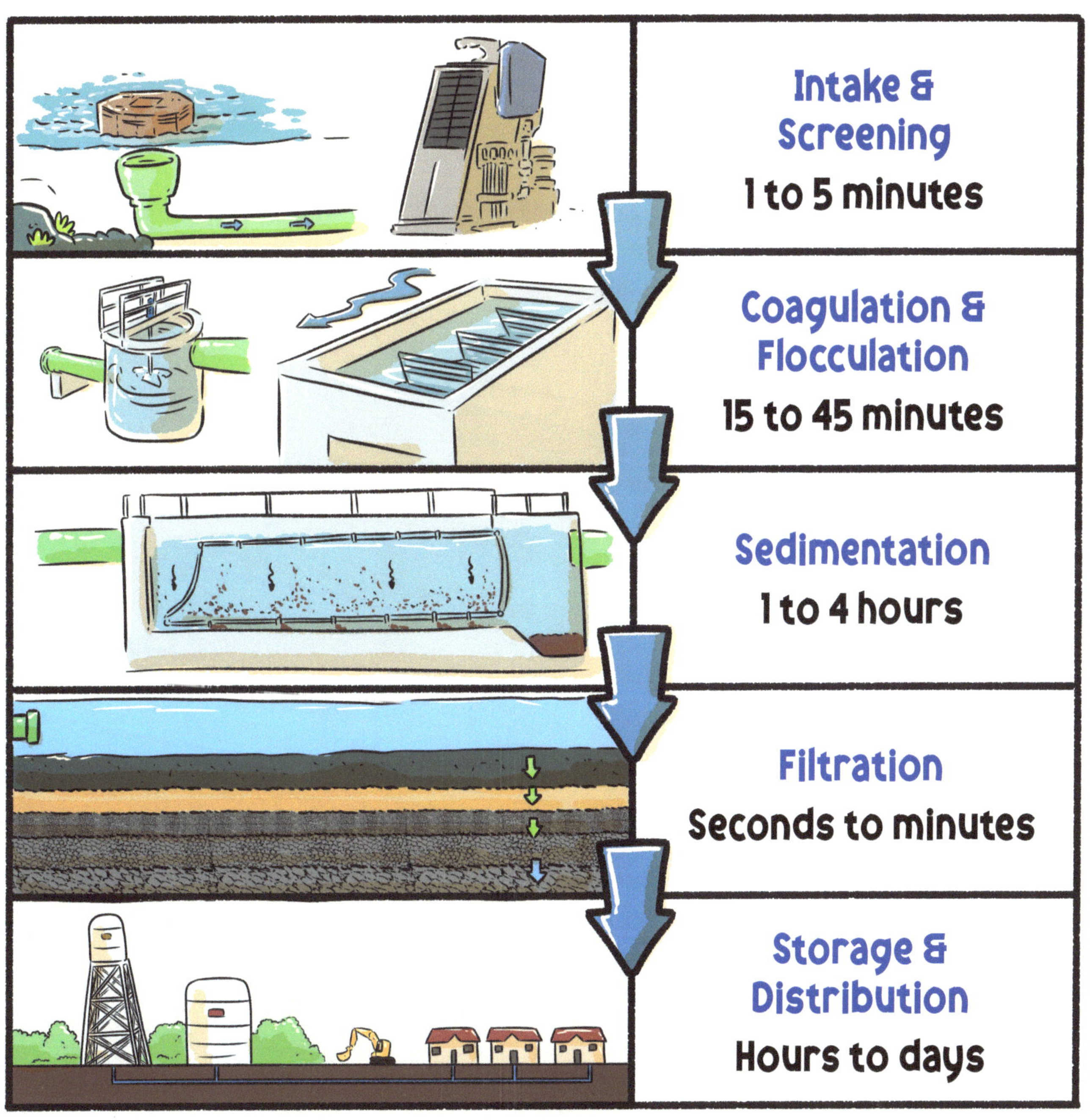

That's how
TAP WATER
works!
40

About the Author

I have been working in the water treatment industry since 1997. I hold a Bachelor of Science degree from Grambling State University and a Master of Science degree from Rosalind Franklin University School of Medicine and Science. Additionally, I possess an Illinois Environmental Protection Agency Class A Water Operator's License.

My career has included the oversight and management of three municipal public water supplies that included two Lake Michigan Class A Conventional Water Treatment Facilities.

I have been actively involved in establishing high school water operator in-training programs across the State of Illinois since 2015, assisting various utilities, schools, and not for profit organizations.

Through the years my colleagues have affectionately and professionally referred to me as

THE WATER KING!

Glossary

Adsorption (ad-SORP-shun):
occurs during the filtration process whereby particles that did not get removed during the sedimentation process are removed by sticking to the surface of the filter media like anthracite.

Aesthetic (ess-THET-ik):
refers to how the tap water tastes, smells, and appears following complete treatment. These attributes are not regulated by the government but can create a negative perception of the water quality by the community.

Aquifer (AK-wuh-fur):
a naturally occurring underground storage tank that holds groundwater. The water in the aquifer can be tapped and used as source water where a public water supply can apply treatment and distribute to the community. Often times ground water is very hard meaning it has a great deal of minerals like calcium and magnesium that must be removed by going through a softening process where the minerals are settled out of the water.

Aluminum (uh-LOO-muh-num) Sulfate (SUL-fayt) Alum (AL-um):
a chemical used during the coagulation stage of the conventional water treatment process that causes colloidal particles in the water to clump together forming a larger and heavier particle that will settle during the sedimentation stage. Colloidal particles possess a negative charge on its surface while alum has a positive charge that neutralizes the negative charge on the colloid particle.

Cationic (kat-eye-ON-ik) Polymer (PAHL-uh-mer):
a chemical that is used in conjunction with alum during the coagulation stage of the conventional water treatment process. The polymer has a positive charge on its surface that is used to neutralize the negative charge on the surface of the colloidal particle.

Cell (sel):
all living organisms have cells that perform various important functions and contain DNA.

Centrifugal (sen-TRIF-yuh-guhl) Pump (puhmp):
an essential piece of equipment used in a water treatment facility that uses energy like electricity to move fluids like untreated water and tap water following proper treatment.

Glossary

Chemical (KEM-ih-kuhl):

substances made of atoms that are used during the conventional treatment process in order to treat the water and comply with government drinking water regulations. Examples of water treatment chemicals include chlorine (disinfection), aluminum sulfate (alum) and polymer that is used for coagulation.

Clearwell (KLEER-well):

underground storage tank located at the water treatment facility where finished tap water is stored prior to pumping it into the water distribution system.

Coagulation (koh-ag-yuh-LAY-shun):

process where water treatment chemicals are used to cause particles in the water to clump together and eventually settle out due to gravity in the sedimentation stage.

Colonization (kah-luh-nuh-ZAY-shun):

hard surfaces like intake structures are ideal locations for quagga mussels to attach to, feed and quickly reproduce (make more quagga mussels). This colonization can restrict the flow of water coming into the water treatment facility to be treated. If this happens the water needed to satisfy the community's demand would not be available.

Conventional (kuhn-VEN-shuh-nuhl) Water (WAH-ter) Treatment (TREET-ment) Process (PRAH-sess):

a conventional water treatment process includes coagulation, flocculation, sedimentation, filtration, and disinfection. This process is over 150 years old and is used to treat the water to ensure the tap water meets drinking water quality standards set forth by the government.

Corrosion (kuh-ROH-zhun) Inhibitor (in-HIB-ih-ter) Chemical (KEM-ih-kuhl):

a chemical that is added to tap water as it enters the water distribution system is used to reduce the corrosion of metal pipes (lead, copper, galvanized) from leaching into the drinking water. Leaching usually occurs when the water has been stagnant in the pipes for six hours or more.

Cryptosporidium (krip-toh-spuh-RID-ee-um):

a parasite that is found in contaminated water. This parasite cannot be removed by the disinfection process and must be removed during the sedimentation process if it is present. This parasite lives in the intestines of animals and humans.

Glossary

Cubic (KYOO-bik) Kilometer (kih-LOM-uh-ter):
a cubic kilometer (km^3) is a unit of volume that measures 1 kilometer (1000 meters) on each side.

Disinfection (dis-in-FEK-shun):
the process of killing harmful bacteria that can be found in water. Disinfection is a required Environmental Protection Agency requirement to ensure tap water can be consumed.

Escherichia (esh-uh-RIK-ee-uh) coli (KOH-lye)/E. coli:
used as part of the drinking water treatment process to determine if the treatment process was effective. Certified laboratory personnel perform the water quality testing of the tap water. If E.coli is detected it indicates contamination which can trigger follow up testing, boil orders, and public notification.

Energy (EN-er-jee):
energy is used during the conventional water treatment process in order to treat the source water. Energy sources such as electricity, natural gas, diesel, and renewable energy sources can be used.

Fecal (FEE-kuhl) coliform (KOH-luh-form):
bacteria that are found in the intestines of animals and humans that can indicate the presence of contaminated water.

Flocculation (flok-yuh-LAY-shun):
a process that follows rapid mixing and precedes sedimentation. Flocculation is a slow mixing of chemicals (coagulants like alum and polymer), water, and particles, that promotes the particles to clump together and become larger and result in settling during the sedimentation process due to gravity.

Friction (FRIK-shun):
resists the flow of water during the filtration process which can result in pressure loss and increase the pressure requirement in order to properly filter and treat the water.

Giardia (jee-AR-dee-uh):
a parasite that can cause an intestinal infection and can be spread as a result of contaminated water.

Gravity (GRAV-ih-tee):
a force that pulls objects towards one another.

Glossary

High-lift (HY-lift) Pump (puhmp):

pumps that moves treated water throughout the public water distribution system, provides system pressure, fills standpipes, and elevated tanks. These pumps are also responsible for providing pressure that can be boosted by firefighters to fight fires. In addition, these pumps provide pressurized tap water to buildings and homes.

Intake (IN-tayk) pipe (pype):

a pipe that has been designed by professional engineers and built in the source water (lake) by a qualified contractor. This pipe is responsible for delivering untreated water to the water treatment facility that will ultimately get treated and pumped throughout the community for use.

Invasive (in-VAY-siv) Species (SPEE-sheez):

animals or plants from another part of the world that have been introduced into a new environment. These species can have a significant negative impact on the new environment.

Loss of head (loss uhv hed)/LOH:

is a key indicator for water plant operators to backwash a filter after it has been in service for a period of time. There is a loss of pressure due to the accumulation of particles that have been removed from the water during the filtration process (adsorption). This accumulation of particles results in the increase of pressure required to perform normal filtration operation which is not ideal for filter performance and integrity.

Low-lift Pump (LOH-lift puhmp):

a pump that moves untreated source water that enters the treatment facility from a lower elevation to a higher elevation to begin the treatment process.

Megawatt (MEG-uh-wot):

a unit of measurement that is equal to one million watts.

Naturally occurring organic matter (NATCH-er-uh-lee uh-KUR-ing or-GAN-ik MAT-er)/NOM:

decaying plants and micro-organisms that are found in water.

Microorganism (MY-kroh-OR-guh-niz-um):

living things like bacteria and viruses that are so small that they can only be seen by using a microscope.

Glossary

Neutralize (NOO-truh-lyze):
a process that can cancel the toxic effects of a chemical like chlorine gas making it harmless.

Organism (OR-guh-niz-um):
an organism is a living thing that can be made up of one or many cells that function on its own, such as a plant, animal, or human.

Parasite (PAIR-uh-site):
an organism that lives in or on another organism and gets its food from it.

Pathogen (PATH-uh-jen):
a microorganism like bacteria or viruses that can cause sickness, disease, and even death.

Potable water (POH-tuh-buhl WAH-ter):
water that has been properly treated, meets drinking water standards, and can be used to drink and for cooking.

Public Water Supply (PUB-lik WAH-ter suh-PLY):
this is the water utility that is responsible for supplying drinking water to the community. Some public water supplies are small, medium, and large. Public water supplies are regulated by the government to meet standards to ensure the water quality being provided to the community.

Pump impeller (puhmp im-PEL-er):
part of a pump with blades that rotate quickly due to being connected to a shaft and motor that uses energy, like electricity, to move a liquid such as water. Both high-lift and low-lift centrifugal pumps have impellers.

Residual (rih-ZIJ-oo-uhl):
this is the level of a chemical that is left over following treatment. When chlorine is added into the water some of it gets used up. The amount that is left over and detectable is the residual.

Sedimentation (sed-uh-men-TAY-shun):
a physical water treatment process that uses gravity to remove the particles from water. 90% or more of the particles are removed during the sedimentation or settling process. Sedimentation precedes the filtration step during the conventional water treatment process.

Glossary

Supervisory Control and Data Acquisition system (SOO-per-vuh-zor-ee kun-TROHL and DAY-tuh ak-wuh-ZIH-shun SIS-tum)/SCADA:
used to monitor and control the conventional water treatment process. This technology is critical for proper decision making for the water plant operators and other facility staff. SCADA systems use hardware and software in order to supervise, control, and acquire data twenty-four hours a day seven days each week.

Surface Tension (SUR-fiss TEN-shun):
contributes to floc formation during the coagulation process which results in removing the particles from water by pulling them together due to van der Waals forces.

Tap-water (TAP WAH-ter):
water that comes out of faucets of a building, such as a house, that is connected to the public water system (distribution system).

Total coliforms (TOH-tuhl KOH-luh-formz):
a group of bacteria that are not harmful to people but are used as an indicator for the potential presence of harmful bacteria such as E. coli. Total coliforms are used to determine the water quality of the treated tap water that is leaving the treatment facility and entering the water distribution system that ultimately delivers tap water to homes and buildings.

Van der Waals Forces (van der WAHLZ FOR-siz):
weak intermolecular forces that play a very important role during the adsorption process where particles in the water following sedimentation stick to the surface of an adsorbent material like anthracite and are removed.

Water (WAH-ter):
a clear, odorless, and tasteless liquid that is essential for life. Water exists in serveral forms such as rain, ice, and vapor.

Water Distribution System Demand (WAH-ter dis-trih-BYOO-shun SIS-tum dih-MAND):
the total amount of water required to meet the needs of a community at a given time.

Water Formula (WAH-ter FOR-myuh-luh):
the formula for water is "H2O", that is made up of two hydrogen atoms and one oxygen atom.

Glossary

Water Pressure (WAH-ter PREH-sher):

in a water distribution system, the minimum water pressure required is 20 psi but can vary from system to system based on various factors such as system design, elevation, and water quality. Maintaining a minimum system pressure is required by the United States Environmental Protection Agency to ensure proper water quality and prevent contamination within the distribution system.

Watt (WOT):

a unit of measurement for power.

Zeta Potential (ZAY-tuh puh-TEN-shuhl):

this is very important during the coagulation and flocculation phases. zeta potential determines whether or not particles will clump together or repel each other. The higher the zeta potential, the more the particles repel each other. The lower the zeta potential the more attracted the particles become. An example of zeta potential is a magnet. When the sides of the magnet with the same charge are brought close to one another, they repel each other. The opposite happens when the sides with different charges (positive and negative) are put together, the magnets stick to each other to form a larger magnet.

Activity

Answer the questions about
"How Does Tap Water Work –
The Conventional Water Treatment Process"?

1. What steps are included in the conventional water treatment process?

2. How is raw water brought in or drawn from the lake?

3. Conventional water treatment cleans the water by removing what?

4. Is Cryptosporidium a parasite?
    True or False

5. Does chlorine kill Cryptosporidium?

6. Quagga mussels were originally found in the United States?
    True or False

7. The low lift pumps are used to move the raw water from the intake wells?
    True or False

8. Do the particles in the lake, called colloids, have negative or positive charges?

9. Are the lake raw water colloid particles attracted to one another or are they repelled by one another?

10. Is the rapid mixing step a short or long process?

11. Which process removes over 90% of the floc?

12. How are the sedimentation basins cleaned out?

13. Do the clearwells store potable or raw water?

14. What are the high lift pumps used for?

15. What is the water called that comes out of the kitchen faucet at home?

16. Is water treated the same way at every water treatment facility?

17. The amount of water pumped throughout the distribution system is determined by what?

18. Name the different sources that water can be taken from?

19. Which agency sets drinking water standards that must be met to protect public health?

20. Name some professionals that help "Make the Tap Water Work"?

Activity - Answers

Answers to the questions about
"How Does Tap Water Work -
The Conventional Water Treatment Process"?

1. This process includes coagulation, flocculation, sedimentation, filtration and disinfection.

2. Intake pipes

3. Particles

4. True

5. No

6. False

7. True

8. Negative charges

9. Repelled by one another

10. Short process

11. Sedimentation

12. The tanks are cleaned out with fire hoses twice a year. The sludge can be disposed of by using a centrifuge or pumped to a wastewater plant for treatment and disposal. The centrifuge separates water from the sludge. The sludge can then be sent to a landfill using large trucks.

13. Potable water

14. The high lift pumps pump the water out of the clearwells to homes, schools, churches, and businesses throughout the community. The high lift pumps also provide pressure that sends the water throughout the community through an underground network of pipes called water mains.

15. Tap water

16. No. Water is not treated the same way everywhere because of the contaminants in the source raw water are different.

17. Demand

18. Some water comes from lakes, rivers, and even the ocean. Others use ground water where it is withdrawn from aquifers.

19. The Environmental Protection Agency

20. There are lots of professionals like: laborers, mechanics, laboratory technicians, water operators, engineers, utility managers, geographic information system technicians, plumbers, customer service specialists, attorneys, financial specialists, and many more that "help the tap water work".